MAGIC CASTLE READERS®

Where Is Baby Bear?

A book about animal homes

BY JANE BELK MONCURE • ILLUSTRATED BY PAIGE BILLIN-FRYE

The Child's World

Published by The Child's World®
1980 Lookout Drive • Mankato, MN 56003-1705
800-599-READ • www.childsworld.com

Acknowledgments
The Child's World®: Mary Berendes, Publishing Director
The Design Lab: Design
Jody Jensen Shaffer: Editing

ISBN 9781623235857
LCCN 2013931348

Printed in the United States of America
Mankato, MN
July 2013
PA02177

Did you know...

A library is a magic castle with many Word Windows in it?

What is a Word Window?

If you said, "A book," you're right!

A book is a Word Window because the words and pictures let you look and see many things. Books are your windows to the wide, wide world around you.

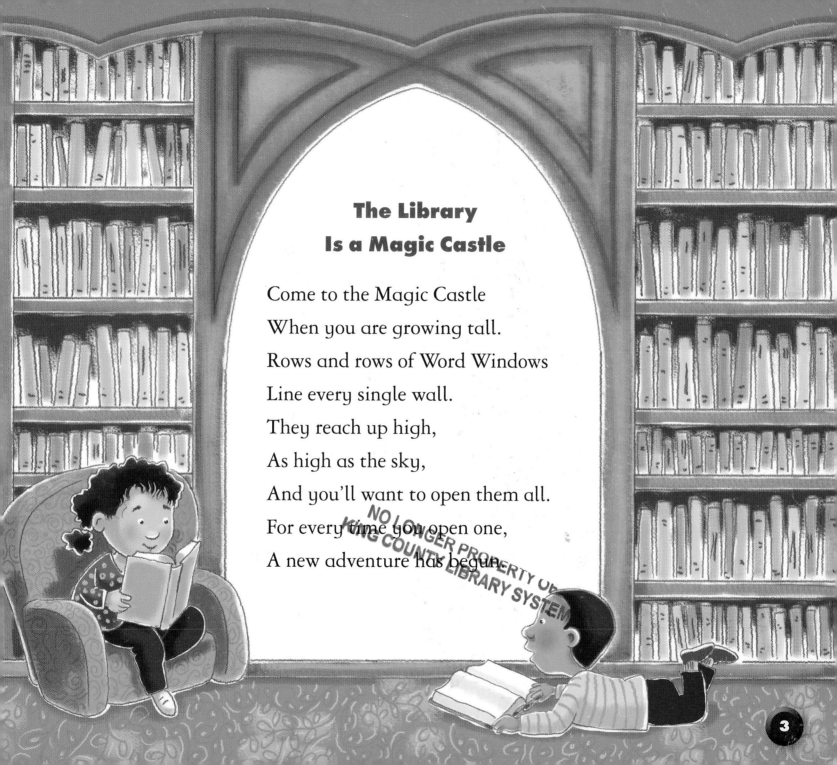

The Library
Is a Magic Castle

Come to the Magic Castle
When you are growing tall.
Rows and rows of Word Windows
Line every single wall.
They reach up high,
As high as the sky,
And you'll want to open them all.
For every time you open one,
A new adventure has begun.

Peter opened a Word Window.
Guess what he saw.

Some animals playing in the woods.

"Will you play with me?" said Peter.

"Yes," said the animals.
"We will play hide-and-seek with you."

"We will hide first. Close your eyes. Do not peek."

And away they ran.

Peter counted to ten.
"Ready or not, here I come!" he said.

"I will find Duck first," said Peter.
He looked behind a tree. Was Duck there?

Peter looked under a big rock.
Was Duck under the rock?

"Maybe Duck went home," said Peter.
Peter ran to the pond.

Peter saw turtles, a frog, and some fish,
but not Duck.

Then Peter looked behind some cattails.
"There you are, Duck! You are at home
in the pond where you belong," said Peter.

"Now I will find Bunny.
Where are you, Bunny?" said Peter.

Peter looked in the barn. Was Bunny in the barn?
"Maybe Bunny went home," said Peter.

Peter ran to the field. He saw bees and
butterflies and grasshoppers, but not Bunny.

Then Peter looked behind some daisies.
"There you are, Bunny! You are at home
in the field where you belong."

"Now I will find Raccoon.
Where is Raccoon hiding?" said Peter.

Peter looked in a cave. Was Raccoon in the cave?
"Maybe Raccoon went home," said Peter.

Peter climbed a tree. He saw baby birds
and a squirrel, but not Raccoon.

Then Peter looked in a hole at the top of the tree.
"There you are, Raccoon! You are at home
in the tree where you belong."

"Now I will find Baby Bear. I will win the game!"
Peter said. He ran to the beach.

Peter looked up and down the beach.
He looked in a boat.
Was Baby Bear hiding there?

"Maybe Baby Bear went home," said Peter.
"But I do not know where Baby Bear lives."
Peter sat down on an old log.

"Where does Baby Bear live?" asked Peter.
Raccoon would not tell.
Duck would not tell.
Bunny would not tell.

"I give up," said Peter.
"Baby Bear wins the game."

Just then, the log began to roll. Everyone fell off.
PLOP!

"Surprise!" said Baby Bear.
"You were sitting on my home. I win the game!"

"Maybe I will win the next time," said Peter.
"Now I must go to *my* home. Good-bye."
Peter closed the Word Window.

Questions and Activities

(Write your answers on a sheet of paper.)

1. Where does this story happen?
   Name two important things about that place.

2. Name two things you learned about animal homes.
   What else would you like to know?

3. Did this story have any words you don't know?
   How can you find out what they mean?

4. Look at the picture on page 30.
   How does it show where Baby Bear's home is?

5. Tell this story to a friend. Take only two minutes.
   Which parts did you share?